AFRICAN WRITERS SERIES

FOUNDING EDITOR Chinua Achebe

A Simple Lust

A Simple Lust

Selected poems including
Sirens Knuckles Boots
Letters to Martha
Poems from Algiers
Thoughts Abroad

Dennis Brutus

HEINEMANN
LONDON · IBADAN · NAIROBI · LUSAKA

Heinemann Educational Books Ltd
22 Bedford Square, London WC1B 3HH
P.M.B. 5205 Ibadan · P.O. Box 45314 Nairobi
P.O. Box 3966 Lusaka
EDINBURGH MELBOURNE AUCKLAND
HONG KONG SINGAPORE KUALA LUMPUR NEW DELHI
EXETER (NH) KINGSTON PORT OF SPAIN

ISBN 0 435 90115 X

Photoset in Malta
by St Paul's Press Ltd
Reproduced, printed and bound in Great Britain by
Cox & Wyman Ltd, London, Fakenham and Reading

Contents

[vii]

PART II LETTERS TO MARTHA

The rearrangement of 'Letters to Martha' and other poems from a South African prison falls into the following divisions: early poems; poems about prison; poems written while under house-arrest; into exile. The order is generally chronological.

[viii]

PART III AFTER EXILE

Acknowledgements

This is the first time that these poems have been collected together. This collection includes four previously published books: *Sirens Knuckles Boots*, *Letters to Martha*, *Poems from Algiers*, and *Thoughts Abroad* by John Bruin. A section of *Seven South African Poets* was by Dennis Brutus. To these are added poems which have appeared in journals, and others which have not been published before.

Poems on pages 1—33 were first published under the title *Sirens Knuckles Boots* (Mbari Publications, Ibadan/Northwestern University Press, Evanston, 1963)

Poems on pages 44—96 were first published under the title *Letters to Martha* (African Writers Series 46, Heinemann, London, 1968)

Poems on pages 139—141 were first published under the title *Poems from Algiers* (African and Afro-American Research Institute, University of Texas, Austin, 1970)

Poems on pages 39—42, 103—106, 116—127, 130—131, 158, 169 were first published under the title *Thoughts Abroad* by John Bruin (Troubadour Press, Del Valle, Texas, 1970)

Poems on pages 35—37, 99, 101—102, were first published in *Seven South African Poets* (African Writers Series 64, Heinemann, London, 1971).

Some of these poems have appeared in various magazines, including the following: *Adelphi*, *African Arts*, *Africa Today*, *Black Orpheus*, *Breakthru*, *Encounter*, *Fighting Talk*, *Disenchanted*, *Common Ground*, *Literary Review*, *Inkululeko*, *The Jewel of Africa*, *The Journal of New African Literature and the Arts*, *New African*, *New Age*, *Presence Africaine*, *Purple Renoster*, *Revolution Africaine*, *The Rag*, *The Observer*, *Okike*, *Transition*, *Western Mail*, *Poetry 1/2 Comment*, *Nexus*, *Zuka*.

One

SIRENS KNUCKLES BOOTS AND OTHER EARLY POEMS

A troubadour, I tráverse all my land
exploring all her wide-flung parts with zest
probing in motion sweeter far than rest
her secret thickets with an amorous hand:

and I have laughed, disdaining those who banned
inquiry and movement, delighting in the test
of will when doomed by Saracened arrest,
choosing, like unarmed thumb, simply to stand.

Thus, quixoting till a cast-off of my land
I sing and fare, person to loved-one pressed
braced for this pressure and the captor's hand
that snaps off service like a weathered strand:
— no mistress-favour has adorned my breast
only the shadow of an arrow-brand.

Take out the poetry and fire
of watch it ember out of sight,
sanity reassembles its ash
the moon relinquishes the night.

But here and here remain the scalds
a sudden turn or breath may ache,
and I walk soft on cindered pasts
for thought or hope (what else?) can break.

Somehow we survive
and tenderness, frustrated, does not wither.

Investigating searchlights rake
our naked unprotected contours;

over our heads the monolithic decalogue
of fascist prohibition glowers
and teeters for a catastrophic fall;

boots club the peeling door.

But somehow we survive
severance, deprivation, loss.

Patrols uncoil along the asphalt dark
hissing their menace to our lives,

most cruel, all our land is scarred with terror,
rendered unlovely and unlovable;
sundered are we and all our passionate surrender

but somehow tenderness survives.

Between the time of falling for the flowers
and lush profusion of the summer's leaves
the trees with naked boughs achieve
an almost-autumn elegance
of delicate austere intricacy:
this is the end of spring, the start of summer
and in this stripped athletic grace
subdued assurance of fresh hope
more certain than the burgeoning of spring
more meaningful than summer's fulsome load.

The Sibyl

Her seer's eyes saw nothing that the birds did not,
her words were sharp and simple as their song;
that mutant winds had honed their teeth on ice
that sap ran viscous in the oaks and senile pines —
these things were common cause except to those
whose guilty fear had made them comatose:
who could not guess that red coagulate stains
would burst from summer's grossly swollen veins
or spell out from the leaves of opulent decadence
that autumn's austere nemesis would come to
    cleanse?

More terrible than any beast
that can be tamed or bribed
the iron monster of the world
ingests me in its grinding maw:

agile as ballet-dancer
fragile as butterfly
I eggdance with nimble wariness
— stave off my fated splintering.

Out of the granite day
a stream of sunlight thrusts
spills over sombre dust:

brightness afar
cascades images
of someone bright and dear
and far away.

This sun on this rubble after rain.

Bruised though we must be
some easement we require
unarguably, though we argue against desire.

Under jackboots our bones and spirits crunch
forced into sweat-tear-sodden slush
— now glow-lipped by this sudden touch:

— sun-stripped perhaps, our bones may later sing
or spell out some malignant nemesis
Sharpevilled to spearpoints for revenging

but now our pride-dumbed mouths are wide
in wordless supplication
— are grateful for the least relief from pain

— like this sun on this debris after rain.

Time — ordinary time —
exerts its own insistent
unobtrusive discipline:
today's undone work is axed
into oblivion by the chores
that thud on it tomorrow
and spit it in the basket of neglect:

and these — these sores —
unhealed and unattended
that bleed afresh each day
under the horny ministrants of law
must, under impulse of augmented streams
explode in gouts and swish
these papered clerks and all
into a messy bloodied waste.

Waiting
(South African Style):
'Non-Whites Only'

1

At the counter an ordinary girl
with unemphatic features and
a surreptitious novelette
surveys with Stanislav disdain
my verminous existence and consents
with langorous reluctance —
the dumpling nose acquiring chiselled charm
through puckering distaste —
to sell me postage stamps:
she calculates the change on knuckly fingertips
and wordless toothless-old-man mumbling lips.

2

Was ever office-tea-coloured tea as good as this
or excited such lingering relishing ever?
Railway schedules hoot at me derision
as trains run on their measured rods of time:
But here in this oasis of my impotence
the hours dribble through lacunae in my guts:
Stoic yourself for some few hours more
till the Civil Service serves — without civility:
'Arsenic and Old Lace' andantes through my head.

[11]

Off The Campus: Wits

Tree-bowered in this quaint romantic way
we look down on the slopes of sunlit turf
and hear the clean-limbed Nordics at their play.

We cower in our green-black primitive retreat
their shouts pursuing us like intermittent surf
peacock-raucous, or wracking as a tom-tom's beat;

so we withdraw from present, place and man
— to green-clad Robin with an iron beak
or Shakespeare lane-leaf-hidden from a swollen
        Anne.

So here I crouch and nock my venomed arrows
to pierce deaf eardrums waxed by fear
or spy, a Strandloper, these obscene albinos
and from the corner of my eye
catch glimpses of a glinting spear.

Autumn comes here with ostentation.
Her polite-shrew's voice is sharp in the wind
she trails her hair,
wind-blown browns in the blonde,
across the oaks, streaking their nervous green:
her gusty breath,
passion-keen,
is sweet in the morning air
intense with the desire for possession
— and for death.

No Banyan, Only

The quiet wisdom of the body's peace:
Carnality, in this our carnal world, is all
Bamboo and iron having sealed
Our mundane eyes to views of time and peace.

Now I am strong as stones or trees are strong,
Insensible, or ignorant with vibrant life;
Streams or the air may wash or pass me by
My mind breathes quiet, lying yours along.

(Upon what meat is this man fed
That he is grown so great?
Diet of eloquent delectable accolades
Warm, soft, kindly, sweet and red.)

Under no banyan tree I strip no onion skin
To find a néant kernel at the still centre:
'A little winter love in a dark corner'?
No, Love (for Chrissake, no) no love, no sin.

Sublunary no more, yet more acutely mundane
    now
Man's fingers claw the cosmos in gestures of
    despair,
Our souls, since Hersey, seek the helix of
    unknowing
Save mine, you-saved, now leafing like a bough.

Breaking through theory-thickets I thrust
To this one corpus, one mere self
That gives Content and content to an earth
Littered and sterile with ideas and rust.

Let alphabetic electronics bloat on Freudian
        excrement,
Our golden bodies, dross-indifferent, count no
        gain,
Finding Gauguin's eternal island afternoon
And you hibiscus and my continent.

Most kindly you and what indeed can be
More most-required than a kindliness
In this our sharded world? And thus
My thanks for heartsease balm you render me.

Animals, perhaps, without merit of their own
— Forgive me Poverello, Paduan, my conceit —
Attain at last such steady ecstasy
As this you give, a gift to make us both your
        own.

Erosion: Transkei

Under green drapes the scars scream,
red wounds wail soundlessly,
beg for assuaging, satiation;
warm life dribbles seawards with the streams.

Dear my land, open for my possessing,
ravaged and dumbly submissive to our will,
in curves and uplands my sensual delight
mounts, and mixed with fury is amassing

torrents tumescent with love and pain.
Deep-dark and rich, with deceptive calmness
time and landscape flow to new horizons —
in anguished impatience await the quickening rains.

At a Funeral

Black, green and gold at sunset: pageantry
And stubbled graves: expectant, of eternity,
In bride's-white, nun's-white veils the nurses gush
    their bounty
Of red-wine cloaks, frothing the bugled dirging
    slopes
Salute! Then ponder all this hollow panoply
For one whose gifts the mud devours, with our
    hopes.

Oh all you frustrate ones, powers tombed in dirt,
Aborted, not by Death but carrion books of birth
Arise! The brassy shout of Freedom stirs our earth;
Not Death but death's-head tyranny scythes our
    ground
And plots our narrow cells of pain defeat and
    dearth:
Better that we should die, than that we should lie
    down.

[*Velencia Majombozi, who died shortly
after qualifying as a doctor*]

Nightsong: City

Sleep well, my love, sleep well:
the harbour lights glaze over restless docks,
police cars cockroach through the tunnel streets;

from the shanties creaking iron-sheets
violence like a bug-infested rag is tossed
and fear is immanent as sound in the wind-swung
      bell;

the long day's anger pants from sand and rocks;
but for this breathing night at least,
my land, my love, sleep well.

The sounds begin again;
the siren in the night
the thunder at the door
the shriek of nerves in pain.

Then the keening crescendo
of faces split by pain
the wordless, endless wail
only the unfree know.

Importunate as rain
the wraiths exhale their woe
over the sirens, knuckles, boots;
my sounds begin again.

It is your flesh that I remember best;
its impulse to surrender and possess
obscurely, in the nexus of my flesh
inchoate stirrings, patterns of response
re-act the postures of our tenderness.

Yet I would contemn myself in guilt
for contumely to you if this were all
for know, as dearly memorable are speech
the shy expressive gestures of your eyes
your patient, penetrative, patient mind.

[*For My Wife, In Separation*]

Mirror Sermon

This cold reflection
of our interlocking nudity
        moralizes ascetically
on sensual intellection
        or mortality.

Our images cavort
in silent dissonance
        or graceless dance
slow sarabands of passionless lasciviousness
and lace through a cacophonous gavotte.

Marionettes
devoid of graceful antecedents
        we pirouette
in senseless choreography
or jerk on twitching strings of lust.

Flat, two-dimensional
deprived of sensual rationalizations
whose warmth can melt the body's aberrations
        and mould them to pretence of sanity,
        these figures twist to new inanity.

Ghouls
bloodless, bodiless, unsouled
        these wraiths unfold,
                grotesque,
        in writhing arabesques

Palely our shapes are seen
till, misted by our panting breath
        they shadow cadaver-green
reveal ourselves, unpassioned and obscene
locked in our macabre dance of death.

A common hate enriched our love and us:

Escape to parasitic ease disgusts;
discreet expensive hushes stifled us
the plangent wines became acidulous

Rich foods knotted to revolting clots
of guilt and anger in our queasy guts
remembering the hungry comfortless.

In draughty angles of the concrete stairs
or seared by salt winds under brittle stars
we found a poignant edge to tenderness,

and, sharper than our strain, the passion
against our land's disfigurement and tension;
hate gouged out deeper levels for our passion —

a common hate enriched our love and us.

The rosy aureole of your affection
extends beyond our urban bounded knowledge
to tangled undergrowths of earlier time:
subtly obscure lymphatics of the flesh
proliferate bright labyrinths of mind
and cobweb-shadow them with primal dusk.

Beyond our focussed shaped projection
to immensities of tenderness defined
like blind protrusion of these searching nipples
shut-eyed in luminous rooms of lust I nuzzle,
loom shadows darker than the dusk of passion
that turn our pinks dust-grey as spider's back.

Beyond your open hungering embrace
yawn other older mouths from oozy shores
and over me, enormous, straddles
the ancient foetus-hungry incubus
that leaves me sprawling, spent, discarded
dry-sucked and shattered as a spider's shard.

It is the constant image of your face
framed in my hands as you knelt before my chair
the grave attention of your eyes
surveying me amid my world of knives
that stays with me, perennially accuses
and convicts me of heart's-treachery;
and neither you nor I can plead excuses
for you, you know, can claim no loyalty —
my land takes precedence of all my loves.

Yet I beg mitigation, pleading guilty
for you, my dear, accomplice of my heart
made, without words, such blackmail with your
        beauty
and proffered me such dear protectiveness
that I confess without remorse or shame
my still-fresh treason to my country
and hope that she, my other, dearest love
will pardon freely, not attaching blame
being your mistress (or your match) in tenderness.

Gaily teetering on the bath's edge
one long bare arm outflung to balance
the sweep of satin flanks and thews
face-level the brown triangular fuzz
grey glistening with a hoar of drops,
'Kiss me!' you cried and 'No!' morosely I.

Etched aloft against the prison-grey light
that filtered through the plastic curtaining
the smooth flesh surging tautly over
the thoracic cage to where the nipples gazed
in blandly unselfconscious innocence,
'Kiss me!' you cried, and 'No!' morosely I,

seeing within the cage the soon too-tired muscle
and all this animal spirit spent,
this emphasis on sheer carnality
re-iteration of mortality
and all immediate joys ephemeral,
angered and wounded, 'No!' and 'No!' I cried.

Anguished passion knots your brows
sharpens your temple's curve with shadows
flickers your tongue beyond your lips
—your nipples fumble for my fingertips.

Through your blue and lucent
unending expanses of air
I pulse with phallic thrust
devouring your contoured loveliness:

the grey and silver wings
        of my affection
over-arch to your horizons.

Let not this plunder be misconstrued:
This is the body's expression of need —
Poor wordless body in its fumbling way
Exposing heart's-hunger by raiding and hurt;

Secret recesses of lonely desire
Gnaw at the vitals of spirit and mind
When shards of existence display eager blades
To menace and savage the pilgriming self:

Bruised though your flesh and all-aching my arms
Believe me, my lovely, I too reel from our pain —
Plucking from you these your agonised gifts
Bares only my tenderness-hungering need.

For Bernice

How delicately the blossoms fall!
Like gauze to clothe and swathe my naked lands,
so delicately the blossoms fall.

How delicate their mauve suffusal!
Like allusions to elusive or illusory perfumes,
so delicate their mauve suffusal.

Scarcely disturbing the jacaranda air!
Descent and elegance distill a fragrance
scarcely disturbing the jacaranda air.

And I observe with nervous hands
how delicately the blossoms fall
and, hesitating, half-approach the parent bole
so delicately the blossoms fall!

Kneeling before you in a gesture
unposed and quite unpractised
—I emphasize, though we need not be assured
for neither could take time to posture
standing always stripped to the very bone
and central wick of our real selves
that burnt simple and vulnerable as flame —

Kneeling before you for a moment,
slipped quite unthinkingly into this stance
—for heart, head and spirit in a single movement
responded thus to some stray facet
of your prismatic luminous self
as one responds with total rhythm in the dance —
I knelt

and answering, you pressed my face against your
        womb
and drew me to a safe and still oblivion,
shut out the knives and teeth; boots, bayonets
        and knuckles:
so, for the instant posed, we froze to an eternal
        image
became unpersoned and unageing symbols
of humbled vulnerable wonder
enfolded by a bayed and resolute maternalness.

Under me
    your living face endures
        pools stare blindly
        muddied by ageless misery:

    descending to you
        in a rage of tenderness
            you bear me
            patiently.

    [*Flying into Kimberley*]

Desolate
Your face gleams up
beneath me in the dusk

abandoned:

a wounded dove
helpless
beneath the knife of love.

So, for the moment, Sweet, is peace
I rest, wave-cradled, safe from emotion's spray
balmed by the shadeless trough, the sun-greened,
    sensed,
unfigured lean-feel of your ocean-self.

Oh I know unrest returns, the scourge —
what love can pelican-peck for long
its own swollen heart for sustenance?
can one shake pain as raindrops from a cape?
can the self, an unprotected mollusc, crawl
free from the past's whorled labyrinths?

Even the thought of pain's return brings pain
a fissure mars the moment's quiet delf:
help me my heart to hold this instant still,
Keep me in quiet's acquiescent curve.

For a Dead African

We have no heroes and no wars
only victims of a sickly state
succumbing to the variegated sores
that flower under lashing rains of hate.

We have no battles and no fights
for history to record with trite remark
only captives killed on eyeless nights
and accidental dyings in the dark.

Yet when the roll of those who died
to free our land is called, without surprise
these nameless unarmed ones will stand beside
the warriors who secured the final prize.

[*John Nangoza Jebe: shot by the police in a
Good Friday procession in Port Elizabeth 1956*]

Lutuli: 10 December 1961

The African lion rouses in his shadowy lair
    and roars his challenge through the clamorous
          earth:
    — its billow blots all discords and all jars.

Hippo and elephant and buffalo without dispute
    go lumbering to the drinking pools:
    — but all the land he views he rules:

From here he pads on sun-picked bone and brittle
          thorn
    sniffing the tawny skies of a new day:
    — power ripples over him like the light of
          dawn.

Miles of my arid earth
rasping dry as smoker's cough and craving
heat, hunger ache in your dusty haze
sighing, heaving, tremulous;

all my seared eyes caress your miles —
boulders that blister, scald and rust —
ranging parched reaches of rutted sands;
coax pastels from your dun and dust

and know the tenderness
of these my reaching hands
can conjure moisture, gentleness
and honey sweetness from your yearning hollows.

Milkblue — tender the moonlit midnight sky;
receive me now my sleeping love.
Lovelaughter — gentle, a luminous glow
arches from circling horizoning hills
to this plain your tremulous breast exposes:

So, gentle and tender I brood and bow
over your scent, your hid springs of mirth
and know
here in this dusk, secret and still
I can bend and kiss you now, my earth.

The springs of the flesh flow slack
and limp and tame and slow
                    what then? what then?

When the surcease of sex is gone
the release of the physical breaker crash
                    what then? what then?

Will the old hunger and loneliness remain
the old unappeasable thirst and need?
will the heartache and yearning for comfort remain
with not even the temporary sexual relief?
                    what then? what then?

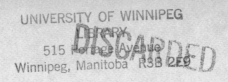
Light, green-yellow luminescent, tender
seeps through these deep-foliaged weeping willows
to filter streams and runnels of soft glow
suffusing enclaves of green and sombre gloom,

and all my frantic and frustrated sorrow
dribbles from me in a pith-central tenderness
extracted by awareness of the charm
that graces this distraught and mourning land.

Oh lacerating land that pulps out anger's
rancid ooze from my resisting heart
now, with this loveliness, you distill in me
a balm that eases and erases all my hurt.

[*Zoo Lake: Johannesburg*]

I might be a better lover I believe
my own, if you could truly be my own:
trafficked and raddled as you are by gross
undiscerning, occupying feet,
how can I, the dispossessed, achieve
the absolute possession that we seek?
How can we speak of infidelity
when, forced apart, we guess each other's woe?
My land, my love, be generous to forgive
my nomad rovings down the vagrant streets:
return to me, sometime be wholly my own
so you secure me entire, entirely your own.

[*Johannesburg*]

I am out of love with you for now;
cold-sodden in my misery
your contours and allurements
cannot move me:

I murmur old endearments to revive
our old familiar glow again
—like sapless autumn leaves
they rasp in vain.

You have asked too much of me:
fond-fool, bereft I cling
unloving, to remembered love
and the spring.

[*Johannesburg*]

When last I ranged and revelled all your length
I vowed to savour your most beauteous curves
with such devout and lingering delight
that they would etch themselves into my brain
to comfort me throughout the prisoned night.

But waking early in the frowsty dawn
and finding you deshevelled and unkempt
my heart arose as though you showed your best
— and then I wryly knew myself to be
the slave of an habituated love.

[*Jbg/Mbabane/Jbg*]

Two

LETTERS TO MARTHA AND OTHER POEMS

Poems

1
Early Poems

Abolish laughter first, I say:
Or find its gusts reverberate
with shattering force through halls of glass
that artifice and lies have made.

O, it is mute now — not by choice
and drowned by multi-choired thunder —
train wails, babies' sirens' wails:
jackboots batter the sagging gate
the wolfwind barks where the tinplate gapes,
earth snarls apocalyptic anger.

Yet where they laugh thus, hoarse and deep
dulled by the wad of bronchial phlegm
and ragged pleuras hiss and rasp
the breath incites a smouldering flame;
here where they laugh (for once) erect —
no jim-crowing cackle for a watching lord,
no sycophant smile while heart contracts —
here laugh moulds heart as flame builds sword.

Put out this flame, this heart, this laugh?
Never! The self at its secret hearth
nurses its smoulder, saves its heat
while oppression's power is charred to dust.

[*Mid-fifties*]
[44]

No, I do not brim with sorrow;
Anger does not effervesce
In viscerally rancid belches
Or burst its bubbles on my optic nerves;
Gall is not secret in my parotids
Nor hatred fetid on my breath:

Only the louse of loneliness
Siphons the interstitial marrows
Of my brain: the inaccessible itch
Mesmerises hands, heart and flesh
Devouring all my scabrous desolate tomorrows.

[*1960*]

Longing

Can the heart compute desire's trajectory
Or logic obfusc with semantic ambiguities
This simple ache's expletive detonation?

This is the wordless ultimate ballistic
Impacting past Reason's, Science's logistics
To blast the heart's defensive mechanism.

O my heart, my lost hope love, my dear
Absence and hunger mushroom my hemispheres;
No therapy, analyses deter my person's fission:

My heart knows now such devastation;
Yearning, unworded, explodes articulation:
Sound-swift, in silence, fall the rains of poison.

[*August 1960*]

Nightsong: Country

All of this undulant earth
heaves up to me;
soft curves in the dark distend
voluptuous-submissively;
primal and rank
the pungent exudation
of fecund growth ascends
sibilant clamorously:
voice of the night-land
rising, shimmering,
mixing most intimately
with my own murmuring —
we merge, embrace and cling:
who now gives shelter, who begs sheltering?

[*April 1962*]

The Mob

[*The white crowd who attacked those who
protested on the Johannesburg City Hall steps
against the Sabotage Bill*]

These are the faceless horrors
that people my nightmares
from whom I turn to wakefulness
for comforting

yet here I find confronting me
the fear-blanked facelessness
and saurian-lidded stares
of my irrational terrors
from whom in dreams I run.

O my people

O my people
what have you done
and where shall I find comforting
to smooth awake your mask of fear
restore your face, your faith, feeling, tears.

[*May 1962*]

Train Journey

Along the miles of steel
that span my land
threadbare children stand
knees ostrich-bulbous on their reedy legs,
their empty hungry hands
lifted as if in prayer.

On The Road

The moon is up; the trees detach
themselves from formless landscapes
to assume a courtly grace,
cloud-bank scatters are light-edged blades
that pale the sparse occasional stars.

The wide night sighs its sensuous
openness, stirring my mind's delight
to a transfiguring tenderness
as stars harden to spearpoint brilliance
and focus fierce demands for peace.

[*January 1963*]

On The Beach

Seablue sky and steelblue sea
surge in cubist turbulence,
dissolve, reform in fluid light
and cadences of sandsharp breeze;

spindrift from sand-dunes tresses down
to inlets where rock-fragments shoal,
seaspray and statice distil the mood
salt-sweet, foamwhite, seaweed-brown.

All in this jagged afternoon
where rock, light, sand and sea-air sing,
brown hair and air-live skin complete
this transitory plenitude.

2

Poems About Prison

Cold

the clammy cement
sucks our naked feet

a rheumy yellow bulb
lights a damp grey wall

the stubbled grass
wet with three o'clock dew
is black with glittery edges;

we sit on the concrete,
stuff with our fingers
the sugarless pap
into our mouths

then labour erect;

form lines;

steel ourselves into fortitude
or accept an image of ourselves
numb with resigned acceptance;

the grizzled senior warder comments:
"Things like these
I have no time for;

they are worse than rats;
you can only shoot them."

Overhead
the large frosty glitter of the stars
the Southern Cross flowering low;

the chains on our ankles
and wrists
that pair us together
jangle

glitter.

We begin to move
    awkwardly.

> [*Colesberg: en route to*
> *Robben Island*]

Letters to Martha
1

After the sentence
mingled feelings:
sick relief,
the load of the approaching days
apprehension —
the hints of brutality
have a depth of personal meaning;

exultation —
the sense of challenge,
of confrontation,
vague heroism
mixed with self-pity
and tempered by the knowledge of those
who endure much more
and endure . . .

2

One learns quite soon
that nails and screws
and other sizeable bits of metal
must be handed in;

and seeing them shaped and sharpened
one is chilled, appalled
to see how vicious it can be
— this simple, useful bit of steel:

and when these knives suddenly flash
– produced perhaps from some disciplined anus –
one grasps at once the steel-bright horror
in the morning air
and how soft and vulnerable is naked flesh.

3

Suddenly one is tangled
in a mesh of possibilities:
notions cobweb around your head,
tendrils sprout from your guts in a hundred
        directions:

why did this man stab this man for that man?
what was the nature of the emotion
and how did it grow?
was this the reason for a warder's unmotived
        senseless brutality?
by what shrewdness was it instigated?

desire for prestige or lust for power?
Or can it – strange, most strange! – be love,
        strange love?
And from what human hunger was it born?

4

Particularly in a single cell,
but even in the sections
the religious sense asserts itself;

perhaps a childhood habit of nightly prayers
the accessibility of Bibles,
or awareness of the proximity of death:

and, of course, it is a currency —
pietistic expressions can purchase favours
and it is a way of suggesting reformation
(which can procure promotion);

and the resort of the weak
is to invoke divine revenge
against a rampaging injustice;

but in the grey silence of the empty afternoons
it is not uncommon
to find oneself talking to God.

5

In the greyness of isolated time
which shafts down into the echoing mind,
wraiths appear, and whispers of horrors
that people the labyrinth of self.

Coprophilism; necrophilism; fellatio;
penis-amputation;
and in this gibbering society
hooting for recognition as one's other selves
suicide, self-damnation, walks
if not a companionable ghost
then a familiar familiar,
a doppelgänger
not to be shaken off.

6

Two men I knew specifically
among many cases:
their reactions were enormously different
but a tense thought lay at the bottom of each
and for both there was danger and fear and pain —
drama.

One simply gave up smoking
knowing he could be bribed
and hedged his mind with romantic fantasies
of beautiful marriageable daughters;

the other sought escape
in fainting fits and asthmas
and finally fled into insanity:

so great the pressures to enforce sodomy.

7

Perhaps most terrible are those who beg for it,
who beg for sexual assault.

To what desperate limits are they driven
and what fierce agonies they have endured
that this, which they have resisted,
should seem to them preferable,
even desirable.

It is regarded as the depths
of absolute and ludicrous submission.
And so perhaps it is.

But it has seemed to me
one of the most terrible
most rendingly pathetic
of all a prisoner's predicaments.

8

"Blue champagne" they called him
— the most popular "girl" in the place;
so exciting perhaps, or satisfying:
young certainly, with youthful curves
— this was most highly prized.

And so he would sleep with several
each night
and the song once popular on the hit-parade
became his nickname.

By the time I saw him he was older
(George *saw* the evil in his face, he said)
and he had become that most perverse among
the perverted:
a "man" in the homosexual embrace
who once had been the "woman".

9

The not-knowing
is perhaps the worst part of the agony
for those outside;

not knowing what cruelties must be endured
what indignities the sensitive spirit must face
what wounds the mind can be made to inflict
        on itself;

and the hunger to be thought of
to be remembered
and to reach across space
with filaments of tenderness
and consolation.

And knowledge,
even when it is knowledge of ugliness
seems to be preferable,
can be better endured.

And so,
for your consolation
I send these fragments,
random pebbles I pick up
from the landscape of my own experience,
traversing the same arid wastes
in a montage of glimpses
I allow myself
or stumble across.

10

It is not all terror
and deprivation,
you know;

one comes to welcome the closer contact
and understanding one achieves
with one's fellow-men,
fellows, compeers;

and the discipline does much to force
a shape and pattern on one's daily life
as well as on the days

and honest toil
offers some redeeming hours
for the wasted years;

so there are times
when the mind is bright and restful
though alive:
rather like the full calm morning sea.

11

Events have a fresh dimension
for all things can affect the pace
of political development –

but our concern
is how they hasten or delay
a special freedom –
that of those the prisons hold
and who depend on change
to give them liberty.

And so one comes to a callousness,
a savage ruthlessness –
voices shouting in the heart
"Destroy! Destroy!"
or
"Let them die in thousands!" –

really it is impatience.

[*11 November 1965*]

[61]

12

Nothing was sadder
there was no more saddening want
than the deadly lack
of music.

Even in the cosy days
of "awaiting trial" status
it was the deprivation
and the need
that one felt most.

After sentence,
in the rasping convict days
it grew to a hunger
— the bans on singing, whistling
and unappreciative ears
made it worse.

Then those who shared one's loves
and hungers
grew more dear on this account —
Fiks and Jeff and Neville
and the others

Strains of Eine Kleine Nachtmusik
the Royal Fireworks,
the New World,
the Emperor and Eroica,
Jesu, joy of man's desiring.

Surreptitious wisps of melody
down the damp grey concrete corridors

Joy.

13

"At daybreak for the isle,"
and
"Look your last on all all things lovely,"
and
"So, for a beginning, I know
there is no beginning."

So one cushions the mind
with phrases
aphorisms and quotations
to blunt the impact
of this crushing blow.

So one grits to the burden
and resolves to doggedly endure
the outrages of prison.

Nothing of him doth change
but that doth suffer a seachange . . .

14

How fortunate we were
not to have been exposed
to rhetoric

— it would have falsified
a simple experience;
living grimly,
grimly enduring

[63]

Oh there was occasional heroic posturing
mainly from the immature
— and a dash of demagogic bloodthirstiness

But generally
we were simply prisoners
of a system we had fought
and still opposed.

15

Extrapolation
is the essential secret of our nature
— or so one may call it:

the capacity
to ennoble
or pervert
what is otherwise
simply animal
amoral and instinctual

and it is this that argues for us
a more than animal destiny
and gives us the potential
for the diabolic
or divinity.

16

Quite early one reaches a stage
where one resolves to embrace
the status of prisoner
with all it entails,
savouring to the full its bitterness
and seeking to escape nothing:

"Mister,
this is prison;
just get used to the idea"

"You're a convict now."

Later one changes,
tries the dodges,
seeks the easy outs.

But the acceptance
once made
deep down
remains.

17

In prison
the clouds assume importance
and the birds

With a small space of sky
cut off by walls
of bleak hostility
and pressed upon by hostile authority
the mind turns upwards
when it can —

— there can be no hope
of seeing the stars:
the arcs and fluorescents
have blotted them out —

the complex aeronautics
of the birds
and their exuberant acrobatics
become matters for intrigued speculation
and wonderment

clichés about the freedom of the birds
and their absolute freedom from care
become meaningful

and the graceful unimpeded motion of the clouds
— a kind of music, poetry, dance —
sends delicate rhythms tremoring through the flesh
and fantasies course easily through the mind:
— where are they going
where will they dissolve
will they be seen by those at home
and whom will they delight?

18

I remember rising one night
after midnight
and moving
through an impulse of loneliness
to try and find the stars.

And through the haze
the battens of fluorescents made
I saw pinpricks of white
I thought were stars.

Greatly daring
I thrust my arm through the bars
and easing the switch in the corridor
plunged my cell in darkness

I scampered to the window
and saw the splashes of light
where the stars flowered.

But through my delight
thudded the anxious boots
and a warning barked
from the machine-gun post
on the catwalk.

And it is the brusque inquiry
and threat
that I remember of that night
rather than the stars.

[20 December 1965]

Postscripts

1

These are not images to cheer you
— except that you may see in these small acts
some evidence of my thought and caring:
but still I do not fear their power to wound
knowing your grief, your loss and anxious care,
rather I send you bits to fill
the mosaic of your calm and patient knowledge
— picking the jagged bits embedded in my mind —
partly to wrench some ease for my own mind.
And partly that some world sometime may know.

2

There are of course tho' we don't see them
— I cut away the public trappings to assert
certain private essentialities —
some heroic aspects of this all
— people outside admire, others pity —
but it is not of these I wish to speak;

but to pin down the raw experience
tease the nerve of feeling and expose
it in the general tissue we dissect;
and then, below this, with attentive ear
to hear the faint heartthrob —
a flicker, pulse, mere vital hint
which speaks of the stubborn will
the grim assertion of some sense of worth
in the teeth of the wind
on a stony beach, or among rocks
where the brute hammers fall unceasingly
on the mind.

[68]

Letters to Martha: Postscripts

3

The seagulls, feathery delicate
and full of grace when flying
might have done much to redeem things;

but their raucous greed and bickering
over a superflux of offal —
a predatory stupidity

dug in the heart with iron-hard beak
some lesson of the nature of nature:
man's ineradicable cruelty?

4

The wind bloweth where it listeth
and no man knoweth whence it came

And we poor temporary mortals
probationary in this vale of tears
damned and blissful in due course
must wait some arbitrary will
to determine our eternal destiny.

5

There were times in my concrete cube
— faceless both the nights and days —
when the arbitrary wind gusted
and I, desolate, realised
on how other things I hung
and how easily I might be damned.

6

A studious highschoolboy he looked
— as in fact I later found he was —
bespectacled, with soft-curved face
and withdrawn protected air:
and I marvelled, envied him
so untouched he seemed to be
in that hammering brutal atmosphere.

But his safety had a different base
and his safely private world was fantasy;
from the battering importunities
of fists and genitals of sodomites
he fled: in a maniac world he was safe.

On The Island
1

Cement-grey floors and walls
cement-grey days
cement-grey time
and a grey susurration
as of seas breaking
winds blowing
and rains drizzling

A barred existence
so that one did not need to look
at doors or windows
to know that they were sundered by bars
and one locked in a grey gelid stream
of unmoving time.

2

When the rain came
it came in a quick moving squall
moving across the island
murmuring from afar
then drumming on the roof
then marching fading away.

And sometimes one mistook
the weary tramp of feet
as the men came shuffling from the quarry
white-dust-filmed and shambling
for the rain
that came and drummed and marched away.

On The Island

3

It was not quite envy
nor impatience
nor irritation
but a mixture of feelings
one felt
for the aloof deep-green dreaming firs
that poised in the island air
withdrawn, composed and still.

4

On Saturday afternoons we were embalmed in
    time
like specimen moths pressed under glass;
we were immobile in the sunlit afternoon
waiting;
Visiting time:
until suddenly like a book snapped shut
all possibilities vanished as zero hour passed
and we knew another week would have to pass.

3
Under House Arrest

For Daantjie—on a New Coin *envelope*

On a Saturday afternoon in summer
greyly through net curtains I see
planes on planes in blocks of concrete masonry
where the biscuit factory blanks out the sky

Cézanne clawing agonisedly at the physical world
wrested from such super-imposed masses
a new and plangent vocabulary
evoking tensions, spatial forms and pressures
almost tactile on the eyeballs,
palpable on the fingertips,
and from these screaming tensions wrenched
new harmonies, the apple's equipoise
the immobility of deadlocked conflicts
– the cramp, paralyses – more rich
than any rest, repose.

And I, who cannot stir beyond these walls,
who shrink the temptation of any open door
find hope in thinking that repose
can be wrung from these iron-hard rigidities.

A Letter to Basil

How deadly an enemy is fear!
How it seeks out the areas of our vulnerability
and savages us
until we are so rent and battered
and desperate
that we resort to what revolts us
and wallow in the foulest treachery.

To understand the unmanning powers of fear
and its corrosive action
makes it easier to forgive.

And there is even room for pity.
For how will you endure
the occasional accusatory voice
in your interior ear,
and how will you, being decent, not sorrow?

[11 November 1965]

Presumably
one should pity the frightened ones
the old fighters
who now shrink from contact:
and it is true I feel a measure of sadness
– and no contempt –
and have no wish to condemn
or even grow impatient

But it is best to shutter the mind and heart
eyes, mouth and spirit;
say nothing, feel nothing and do not let them know
        that they have cause for shame

For Bernice

You were the still oasis
in a whirling vortex
(though it would surprise you)
and I rested with such content
in the thought of you
and our relationship:
true, it was not perfection,
but there seemed to be a shared richness
and you could make such chords of sensibility
sing in me
and permit them resonance
in the chamber of your listening self
that thinking of you
I was simply glad.

Blood River Day

[*For Daphne Edmondson*]

Each year on this day
they drum the earth with their boots
and growl incantations
to evoke the smell of blood
for which they hungrily sniff the air:

guilt
drives them to the lair
of primitiveness
and ferocity:

but in the dusk
it is the all pervasive smell of dust
the good smell of the earth
as the rain sifts down on the hot sand
that comes to me

the good smell of the dust
that is the same
everywhere around the earth.

[*16 December 1965*]

The impregnation of our air
with militarism
is not a thing to be defined
or catalogued;
it is a miasma
wide as the air itself
ubiquitous as a million trifling things,
our very climate;
we become a bellicose people
living in a land at war
a country besieged;
the children play with guns
and the schoolboys dream of killings
and our dreams are full of the birdflight of jets
and our men
are bloated with bloody thoughts; inflated sacrifices
and grim despairing dyings.

Their Behaviour

Their guilt
is not so very different from ours:
— who has not joyed in the arbitrary exercise of
     power
or grasped for himself what might have been
     another's
and who has not used superior force in the
     moment when he could,
(and who of us has not been tempted to these
     things?) —
so, in their guilt,
the bared ferocity of teeth,
chest-thumping challenge and defiance,
the deafening clamour of their prayers
to a deity made in the image of their prejudice
which drowns the voice of conscience,
is mirrored our predicament
but on a social, massive, organised scale
which magnifies enormously
as the private deshabille of love
becomes obscene in orgies.

[*Blood River Day 1965*]

For X.B.

It is a way of establishing one is real;
personal, intimate and civilised:
to shout, be violent or importune
will not do in this context,
but a confrontation, male-female,
is possible, even if not legitimate or moral:
so one hopes, strives, speculates:
it is the wish to be accepted as a person
– something real and living.

For E.C.

Equipoise
Like this is rare,
And thus your gifts are doubly dear:
Intellect moves strong and clear
Nobly matched by nature —
Enchanting fusion, grave and fair!

I

Our aims our dreams our destinations

Thought reconstructed in vacuity

A dialogue:
But God doesn't answer back.

Say then we fear
we hope
we speculate
prognosticate,
what intractable arguments
coil round us
wrestle us Laocoön-like,
and what unnameable horrors
ultimate despair
shudder
and owl-moan hollowly
at the unseen ends
of the dark corridors of the brain.

There looms the threat —
a tight knot forming in the viscera —
of defiant rebellion
so of self-elected damnation —
the only kind a benignant God
makes feasible
— so one feels it
in the tenuous proliferate tendrils of thought.

Well if He damn me,
drive me to damnation
by inflicting the unendurable,
force me along the knife-blades till I choose
perdition
how shall I feel guilty?
When my sense of justice says
He drove me
He damned me
He's the guilty one
and if He chose —
BE DAMNED TO HIM

And then to spend eternity
eternally in revolt
against injustice-justice
fighting in vain
against injustice
in the service of my private justice
against a God turned devil
hoping forever for the triumph of despair.
"Evil be thou my Good."

II

The inherent impulse to good
an inbuilt aspiration
integrated
impossible of disentanglement;
what does it argue?

Is it the seed
from which man grows to divinity
– and, before it,
can God stand condemned?

Before what superior standards
is God found inadequate
His mercy finite and inferior to our own?

And where does compassion
degenerate into sentimentality?

(Pity me! Pity me God! I cry
And imply, not mercy
but a fellow-feeling;
and so?
Impute to him equality
or denigrate his super-humanity
and make it inferior to our own?)

(But he was human once –
or so we are assured
and so can find no human state
beyond the range of his experience
or knowledge:
– but always other depths remain
obscurities of knowledge
divine protectedness,
insulations from our woe)

So we must grapple.

And agony
engenders desperation;

then agnosticism;

then, perhaps
an agonised truth
(truthfulness)

Is He the Infinite Hangman?
Executioner?
Torturer?

Must we be driven to the edge,
racked on the precipice of the world?

For what dread guilt
are these dread exactions made,
the extortion of blood and sighs?

Can we find hope
in thinking that our pain
refines us of our evil dross,
prepares us for a splendid destiny?

or in a fellow-link
a shared enterprise
the splendid Gethsemane
which must purchase redemption for the world
and by our agony
pay debts to buy
the pardon for the world

suffering humanity!
transfigured humanity!
Ecce homo!

[*1 March 1966*]

One wishes for death
with a kind of defiant defeatism

wishing that the worst may befall
since the nearly-worst has so often befallen:

it is not a wish for oblivion
but a pugnacious assertion of discontent

a disgust at the boundless opprobrium of life
a desperation; despair.

[*2 July 1966*]

Steeling oneself to face the day
girding one's self for the wrap of clothes
bracing oneself for the thrust of the world
one buckles to buttons and zips and belts:
With the gritted reluctance and indifference to
      pain
with which one enters an unsought fight
one accepts the challenge the bullying day thrusts
      down.

Let me say it

for no-one else may
or can
or will
or dare

I have lashed them
the marks of my scars
lie deep in their psyche
and unforgettable
inescapable.

Of course there were others who served
and much that I could not have done
but I am a part of the work
and they connect it with me

they know I have done them harm

they who are artists in deprivation
who design vast statutory volumes
and spend their nights in scheming deprival

I have deprived them

that which they hold most dear
a prestige which they purchased with sweat
and for which they yearn unassuagedly
— their sporting prowess and esteem
this I have attacked and
blasted
unforgettably.

The diurnal reminders excoriate their souls

Amid a million successes
— the most valued on fronts where they were under attack —
they grimace under the bitter taste of defeat

their great New Zealand rivals
the Olympic panoply and Wembley roar
for them these things are dead
are inaccessible
unattainable

nowhere else does apartheid exact so bitter a price
nowhere else does the world so demonstrate its disgust
in nothing else are the deprivers so deprived.

And they know I will do more.

What wonder such gingerly menacing claws,
they would rend me if they could
(and perhaps will)
but I accept their leashed-in power
and the cloaked malice of their gaze
and wait

anger and resolution
yeast in me
waiting for the time of achievement
which will come if God wills
when I flog fresh lashes across these thieves.

[*2 July 1966*]

The companionship of bluegum trees
their sheen and spangle against the midday
        winter sun
and the companionable nudge of my heart
knocking against my mind and memory
with evocation of my student hazy days
condemns me once again
labels me poet dreamer troubadour
unreal unworldly muddle-headed fool
while the trees nod and swagger
and the level sunlight flows.

[*8 July 1966*]

After the entertainment
the couples go to bed
their senses sharp to just the pitch
for erotic excitement,
husband and wife
with tastes aroused by shared delight
lover and beloved merged in the glow of sensation
lesbian, jaded boss and para with their various
      thrills
licit or illicit with a special added touch;
after the entertainment
Beethoven with his sonorous percussive exultation
veldfiring to the scored climactic roar
or the stripteaser with a special grossness
thrusting obscenities to the furtherest act
her shouting viewers urged her to;
after the current ballet, premiered show
the bawdy singer in the cabaret
the coupling couples turn to bed.

[*11 July 1966*]

Prayer

O let me soar on steadfast wing
that those who know me for a pitiable thing
may see me inerasably clear:

grant that their faith that I might hood
some potent thrust to freedom, humanhood
under drab fluff may still be justified.

Protect me from the slightest deviant swoop
to pretty bush or hedgerow lest I droop
ruffled or trifled, snared or power misspent.

Uphold — frustrate me if need be
so that I mould my energy
for that one swift inenarrable soar

hurling myself swordbeaked to lunge
for lodgement in my life's sun-targe —
a land and people just and free.

[*3 July 1966*]

4
Into Exile

[*For Canon L. John Collins*]

Now that we conquer and dominate time
hurtling imperious from the sun's laggard slouch
transcendentally watching the Irish jigsaw
slip astream dumbly under masking cloud,
green England dissolved in history-grey
and fanatic old Yeats made mellow by height,

now that all canons of space-time are dumb
and obey the assertions of resolute will
and an intricate wisdom is machined to leash
ten thousand horses in world-girdling flight,
how shall we question that further power
waits for a leap across gulfs of storm;

that pain will be quiet, the prisoned free,
and wisdom sculpt justice from the world's
     jagged mass.

[*5 August 1966*
En route from London to New York
El Al Airlines]
[95]

Above us, only sky
below, cloud
and below that
cloud;
below that
sea;
land is abolished,
only the sky and air and light
a beatific approximation
achieved.

After this power
this conquest of brute reality
what can we not not do
not abolish?

Peace will come.
We have the power
the hope
the resolution.
Men will go home.

> [5 August 1966
> *In flight over the Atlantic*
> *after leaving South Africa*]

Three

AFTER EXILE

Over the thunder-heads of terror we may fly
as now I probe their structure from head to base
from the Thor-hammerhead of their crown
thrashing through their configuration
like a sexually masterful invasion:

and if there is power and grace for this,
then I dare believe there will be ways
to find so great a height and peace
without the thunderclaps and storms
that will burst my land with cataclysmic blood.

Crossing the English coast
returning,
is a synthetic joy;
and synthesized:

the paper-thrillers
of those perennial English wars,
planes limping back to base
after the well-done mission —
wreaking unanalyzable destruction

battered ships
rigging torn and masts askew
salt with long voyaging —
pillage, carronading, slaving —
hove in some quiet fishing village

the sporting hero from the victorious tour
sighting the welcome coastline,
or the fortune-seeker seamed and scarred
returning to the country greenery
the family home half-hidden among trees:

romance and glamour stir —
'faint horns of elfland blowing'
synthetic, synthesized, amalgammed feeling
ringing in a phrase unshaped, unsinging,
that sings unbidden in my sounding head.

In the dove-grey dove-soft dusk
when the walls softened to frozen smoke
and their rigidity melted
receding to miles,
when the air was alive and tender
with a mist of spray from the sea,
the air luminous
and the sky bright with the dulling glimmer
of cooling molten lead;
when the island breathed —
trees, grass, stones and sand breathing
quietly at the end of the long hot day —
and the sea was a soft circling presence —
no longer a tight barbed menacing ring:
in the dusk
nothing was more agonizing than to be seized
by the poignant urgent simple desire
simply to stroll in the quiet dusk:
as I do now:
as I do now, and they do not.

I walk in the English quicksilver dusk
and spread my hands to the soft spring rain
and see the streetlights gild the flowering trees
and the late light breaking through patches of
  broken cloud
and I think of the Island's desolate dusks
and the swish of the Island's haunting rain
and the desperate frenzy straining our prisoned
  breasts:
and the men who are still there crouching now
in the grey cells, on the grey floors, stubborn
  and bowed.

November sunlight silvers my grimy panes,
suffuses the gruel-grey sky
and gleams on the cold woodwork;

such wan luminescence
might as well not be,
lacks all virtue, is devoid of warmth

while Southwards in a steady blaze
like a sheet of molten lead heat pours down
and the world glows, while here I pine.

It is hers, England's, seducing charms
I fear
more than anything else

Why should one not grow comfortable
curled in her so-comfortable embrace

—and then she has such tricks of charm
dear quirks of lovelinesses to enchant:

I must be dourly stubborn in my love
for an arid eroded dust-bowl of a love

Her loveliness tainted by disease
and her best image ravaged and austere

I must be faithful to a land
whose rich years, unlike England's, lie ahead.

[*Airport bus to Arlanda: Stockholm*]

At last the roses burn
red flames and orange,
tea-rose pink and white
smouldering in the dark foliage
in the dark-green lustrous leaves:
the world is ripening and abundant
replete with its joyous growth
while my heart, unseasonal, grieves.

[*London*]

I am the tree
creaking in the wind
outside in the night
twisted and stubborn:

I am the sheet
of the twisted tin shack
grating in the wind
in a shrill sad protest:

I am the voice
crying in the night
that cries endlessly
and will not be consoled.

I must conjure from my past
the dim and unavowed spectre of a slave,
of a bound woman, whose bound figure pleads
    silently,
and whose blood I must acknowledge in my own:

fanciful wraith? imagining?
Yet how else can I reconcile
my rebel blood and protest
but by acknowledgement
of that spectre's mute rebellious blood.

'Bury the great duke'
I piped from the floor
among my cotton reels:

'Yes?' he turned in surprise
and 'Go on' he prompted gently
towelling the lather from a half-shaved cheek:

'Bury the Great Duke
with a noise of lamentation'.

But I faltered while he waited
and until he turned away.

And what other failures over ages
kept him turning half-away?

Today in prison
by tacit agreement
they will sing just one song:
Nkosi Sikekela;
slowly and solemnly
with suppressed passion
and pent up feeling:
the voices strong and steady
but with tears close and sharp
behind the eyes
and the mind ranging
wildly as a strayed bird
seeking some names to settle on
and deeds being done
and those who will do the much
that still needs to be done.

[*26 June 1967*
South African Freedom Day]

. . . And some men died
in agony and dishonour
before they could see this time,
and others are blinded by rheum,
sink dissolutely in their own vomit,
and ambition scales the eyes
of those who wallow in success;
and some now living will not live
to see a new sunlight, with other shadows,
with the scab-shanties bleached to remembered
      scars.

Ought we to walk on the bruised grass
patient, most patient, in the searing cold
grimly — sere yellow, burnt-dun — enduring
the winter's weight, its uniform load?

Ought we to add our personal inflictions
— while men lie on concrete
or fumble stones with torn hands
or sigh their cold breath
in the cold unlighted night?

To be thrown outward in a steel projectile
to hurtle outward in quivering uncertainty
to a cold fragment of a continental ledge
for huddling and perching and grubbing
and ultimately, unthinkably, to find settlement
        there

and huddling in this grey tubular box
to find a gathering of the dispersed frantic
        consciousness
a ragged and stretched fabric of torn anxious
        mind
no longer struggling to encompass a host of
        contingencies
but thoughts roosting, still fluttering, on
        the central branched mind

and anger congeals and becomes aware
partly as the conscious rationale for flight
and partly as the self-conscious indignant
        pose —
the wounded 'banneling', the D.P.-type
who is our age's mendicant and jew

anger too that in its artifice holds off
the true deep wound that lies
like the dark bruised pulp at the heart of the
        fruit:
the agony the heart and mind hold in suspense
the whirling axe — or propeller-blade — whose
        fierceness makes it invisible:

then to alight on green placid earth
to normality and efficient unhostile people
the engines, and all throbbing straining
    stilled
and all things quiet, except the dull half-heard
    throb in the heart . . .

    [*For James Cooke
    arrived from South Africa on an exit permit.*]

In the jungle of our distress
stripe-flanked we champ
and chafe against the bars
of our guilty anxious knowledge:
or writhe in the arid dust of discontent
shouldering, bruising against the thought
of the many other anxious suffering ones.

Dismay wrenches the heart
fissures and heels the fragments;
failure and defeat coalesce,
and woe thrusts down the gut:

and I turn in my sad chagrin
grope for the vague consoling teat
of words, articulation, verse:

this is not my rightful world
here I am simple, naïve, an oaf,
now I must sadden, turn to retreat
unless I recover some stubborn will.

[*Kitwe*]

Fry's still sell chocolate
still glean the cocoabean
and the bean still coalesces a swollen gleam —
sweatdrops globed on salt black flesh,
lambent like blooddrops fresh and red

A factory sprawls in acres of verdant park
and the city squats as it anciently did
on its excremental guilt and dominance —
and a ragged refuse dump of spilled, screwed,
    dried, twisted, torn and unforgiven
        black lives.

    [*Bristol*]

Blue pools of peace
high-basined in the snow-flung Alps —
beyond the cold, sharp and stony ridges,
the stony shouldered ridges:

another day,
another milestone-journey, milestone day,
a sense of expiring years,
of fated cycles, expired chances and lost grace:

and a dogged thrusting-on
to new places, new names and new marks:
so we carve structures,
so we leave striations in the rocks.

[*Crossing the Alps: London — Rome*]

Black hills surround Belfast city
and the town is cold stone
— redstone and grey
in the sharp clear winter air:

here they breed hard men
and a stony history cuts them sharp;

but the young, who have seen firebright nights
and felt the cutting edge of glass and steel
are warm and fiery
with a dear-won human fire.

[*Belfast*]

Eight years in exile

and the years kneaded
from the bruised and quivering mind
such ardour and such sensitivity.

A long agony of passion
banked a great furnace of resolve
that wrought stone dream and marble flower.

Eight years.

[*The Taj Mahal, Agra: New Delhi*]

In the comparative calm of normalcy
my role is tension.
As on this sun-silvered day
the shirt-sleeved leisured float
in a lucent crystal ambience
while strong tides viper through the placid sea.

[*Dubrovnik*]

I am alien in Africa and everywhere:

in Europe, outside Europe I stand and assess them
—find French racial arrogance and Teuton
      superiority,
mouldering English humbug:

and in Africa one finds
chafing, through bumbling,
at the restraints of restraint,
brushing impatiently through varied cultures
in fruitless search of depths:
only in myself, occasionally, am I familiar.

    [Paris —Algiers]

At an edge
the track ends:

drifts of future lie
beyond the precipitous slopes of time

new routes await choosing;
also the menace of half-sensed peaks:

a gracious wisdom
determines, helps acceptance:

new perils perhaps:
from the debris of defeat one crawls
emerges debouching on a vaster plain of challenge.

[*Grenoble*]

Under the Fijian moon
in the sultry pre-dawn dark
a concord of memories murmurs
echoes old longings, misty passions
and new stirrings rustle the sibilant dark.

[*Nandi, Fiji*]

Off to Philadelphia in the morning
after blueberry pancakes U.S.A.
with silver images of people
wrestling the racial problem
flickering on my retina-screen;

outside the shark limousines glide
past neons, glass and chrome,
on 42nd nudies writhe
their sterile unproductive lust;

off to Philadelphia in the morning
to rehearse some moulded and half-singing words,
remouth some banal platitudes
and launch-lodge some arrows
from a transient unambitious hand,
a nerveless unassertive gripe.

[New York]

Through the midnight streets of Teheran
with labours waiting for me
labour and unassuagable desire
and loneliness
I spin out my fated web —
old Ahasuerus of unrevealed destiny —
reeling doggedly in the corridors of
      circumstance
impelled by an impersonally benign
uncaring supernal omniscience.

    [Teheran]

Here
on another island
within sound of the sea
I watch the moon turn yellow
or a blurred Orion heel

And remember
the men on the island
on strips of matting
on the cold floor
between cold walls
and the long endless night.

[*Nelson, New Zealand*]

Shakespeare winged this way using other powers
to wrest from grim rock and a troubled student-
    lad
an immortality outlasting all our time
and hacking out an image of the human plight
that out-endures all facets of half-truth:

here now we hurtle north-east from the westering
    sun
that follows, plucks out from afar
the wingstruts crouched and sunlit for a plunge:

O might I be so crouched, so poised, so hewed
to claw some image of my fellows' woe
hacking the hardness of the ice-clad rock,
armed with such passion, dedication, voice
that every cobblestone would rear in wrath
and batter down a prison's wall
and wrench them from the island where they rot.

    [*Flying to Denmark*]

Orion hunts endlessly
an evanished prey

but here
by the still Adriatic
where Dubrovnik sleeps its medieval dream
away
wavelaps throw starglints
in momentary, fragmentary gleams:

a near —
Narcissus,
here
should he but pause,
Orion might be less inconsolable:
Could he but pause.

Orion hunts an evanished prey
endlessly.

And the hours drag

Peonies droop in the loggia;
curl at the edges and wither,
turn a bruised black and decay:

the hours skein in tight coils,
the multi-millioned hours and the years,
and coil to a power and thrust:

the accumulated effort and energy,
the brooding and impulse and steady drive
bind and ferment and yeast for unleashing:

beneath this laboured furling seed breeds.

I must lug my battered body
garbage-littered
across the frontiers of the world,
recite my wear-shined clichés
for nameless firesides
and fidget, a supple suppliant, for papers
in a thousand wooden ante-rooms;
wince, in the tense air of recognition
as the clean-limbed, simple and innocent grow
      hostile;
— in my baggage I bear the ticking explosives
of reproach, and threat, and challenge.

[*Epping, Sydney*]

I yearn towards the heaving earth
to the mountain-mounds upthrust through
      cloud-veils
and the lace-fringed lilypad islands floating
in the calm lake of our blue Mediterranean:
all the world is mine and to love
and all of its humankind.

[*Across the Mediterranean: Cairo to Frankfurt*]

Landscape of my young world!
Land of soft hills and huts
of aloes and grey-green dreaming firs;
these are the images to lacerate,
against which I glass myself in distance
or a rebellious walling of reserve.
Heartbreaking hillsides and green slopes!
There is no armour to exclude your poignancy,
no blunting, and for me no ease.

In the night, in my mind
memories lurk, and words;
images so sharp, they slash the eyeballs,
clawed, or like tines;
and words, jagged as cut cans
lacerating my hands, and the corners of my mouth;
so I hold off from them in the dark
— recoil from their tearing and their balm
— as one senses — half sees — pink nipples
strain through some diaphanous allure.

Here by the pool my scarred ungainly body
    shrinks,
by blue glass depths, kittenish tinkling ripples
I cool my parched rigid spirit
with anticipations of champagne.

To lift, this once, the foaming goblet
in harsh joy, bright, brittle, unbending as
    glass
while in sere patches of the scraggly well-loved
    grass
in a loneliness desperate and vast
as shooting-star scatterings in glaucous space
for this one guest at least
they thrust down a mute empty glass.

Shatter underfoot
in a weaving of sorrow and joy
nuptial and lamentation,
the pitiful unprotesting glass
reciting the ambivalent Prothalamion:

'If I forget thee, Oh Jerusalem
where by sad waters I sit down remembering'

let the glass-hard longing, anger, pain
shimmer and scintillate awhile
the bright drops of joy-wine gush
while the sharp bright edge of action waits
and fury slakes her thirst a space.

Celebrate the fierce joy of victory
and necessary wounding
that the day may sooner come
of our unexiling:
of our return.

[*Teheran, May 1968*]

Sometimes a mesh of ideas
webs the entranced mind,
the assenting delighted mental eye;
and sometimes the thrust and clash
of forged and metalled words
makes musical clangour in the brain;
and sometimes a nude and simple word
standing unlit or unadorned
may plead mutely in cold or dark
for an answering warmth, an enlightening
        sympathy;
state the bare fact and let it sing.

I *am* the exile
am the wanderer
the troubadour
(whatever they say)

gentle I am, and calm
and with abstracted pace
absorbed in planning,
courteous to servility

but wailings fill the chambers of my heart
and in my head
behind my quiet eyes
I hear the cries and sirens

Finding this rubbish, this debris, of mine
after I am dead,
when they come to pry
mouse-rustling in my papers,
ghoulishly-hopeful in my things,
what rubbish they will find!

Will I shrivel, inanimate, in my shame?
Will the dead flesh curl up in protest
being assessed by curious strangers' hands?

Oh I am filled with horror
now:
then I will lie with misleading calm
— as now I persist
with misleading calm.

In the sunlight
in the roads along the sea
they sell the pale-green streaked and patterned watermelon
with its smooth and tepid skin;
blue Algerian sky and blue Mediterranean sea:
and by Clifton, Sea Point and the Cape.

[*Algiers*]

Only in the Casbah
in its steep, stepped and narrow ways
warrening in shops, homes and passages
past the refuse and the children
and the shrivelled tenacious dames;
only in the Casbah
where the bombed structures gape
in mute reminder of the terror of the French
is the tenacious, labyrinthine and unshatterable
        heart
of resistance
truly known.

   [*Algiers*]

And I am driftwood
on an Algerian beach
along a Mediterranean shore

and I am driftwood.

Others may loll in their carnal pool
washed by tides of sensual content
in variable flow, by regulated plan

but I am driftwood.

And the tides devour,
lusts erode the shelving consciousness
fierce hungers shark at the submerged mind
while the quotidian battering spray . . .

Even the seabird questing
weaving away and across
the long blue rollers coasting
from green shelves of shore-land
and rock-tipped banks,
even the seabird has a place of rest —
though it may vary by season or by tide
and a mate brooding with swollen nares and puffed
          breast
signalling nest-routes with tender secret cries
though it vary by season or by tide.

But I am driftwood
by some white Algerian plage.

And the riptides rip and tear
erode, devour
and unrest, questing, yeasts in my querying
    brain
and I beat on the fierce savaging knowledge
rampaging through my existence
accepting the knowledge, seeking design

For I am driftwood
in a life and place and time
thrown by some chance, perchance
to an occasional use
a rare half-pleasure on a seldom chance

and I grate on the sand of being
of existence, circumstance
digging and dragging for a meaning
dragging through the dirt and debris
the refuse of existence
dragging through the diurnal treadmill of my
    life.

And still I am driftwood.
Still the restlessness, the journeyings, the
    quest,
the queryings, the hungers and the lusts.

(Though we know how clouds gather and have weighed
        the moon,
though we have erected and heaved ourselves
in some vast orgasmic thrust
to be unmundane and to trample the moon —
still the blind tides lunge and eddy,
still we writhe on some undiscovered spit,
coil in some whirlpool of undefinable tide)

Yet in the unmarked waters I discern
traceries of patterns like wisps of spume
where I have gone
and snailtrails in seasands on a hundred shores
where I have dragged my sad unresting loins
—tracks on a lunar landscape that suggest some
        sense —

And still I am driftwood
on some sun-soaked plage.

        [*Club des Pins/Algiers/en route to Paris*]

The home of the brave
and the land of the free
to massacre:

the land of liberty
and freedom of choice
of subjection for others:

the land of plenty
and quality education
for people of quality:

Amerika the beautiful
cesspool.

*'These plants produced enough plutonium to
end the world in one incandescent flash'**

I return to the seething earth
heading northward,
swinging from the South

(where Death, a golden timekeeper
squints telescopically at our vulnerability
and once erupted his logic
through our placid insanity)

swinging westward through an eastward loop
to the big love field
'Big D' boasting of a giant penis,
giant love

---

*From an article in *The Sunday Times* (London) February 8th, 1970, by Cal McCrystal
(New York) quoting from an article to appear in *Environment*, the official publication
of the Scientists' Institute for Public Information. Further quotes: '"The most dangerous
tombs in the world." Vast underground tombs in Washington State, Columbia, holding
as much radioactivity as would be released in a nuclear war, are vulnerable to earth-
quakes, two geologists warn America in a forthcoming report. The 140 storage tanks at
the Atomic Energy Commission's reservation at Hansford hold high-level radioactive
wastes with a life of hundreds of thousands of years . . . most of the Hansford reactors
are now shut down but, says *Environment*, during their years of operation, "these plants
produced enough plutonium to end the world in one incandescent flash" . . . The Waste
Solidification Engineering Prototype went into operation in 1966. . . . by last June it had
processed . . . possibly less than one per cent. "At this rate", says *Environment*, "it will
be centuries before the entire accumulation is solidified."' Other references in the poem
are to a multiple shooting at the University of Texas at Austin, the Kennedy assassin-
ation in Dallas, and the Rocky Flats fire (Atomic Energy Commission plant) near Denver.

D.B.

(where Death's fell missile darted
beamed on a telescopic focus of light
on a vulnerable nape, raying like light
in the proud defenceless meat

—for the potentially healing must die
lest they obstruct the midas-change
of all things to fatality
in this doomed micro-mini-universe)

and west and north to the range
the continental divide,
the upthrust complaisant mound
the outflung, submissive, earth;

further north the earth boils
and on the nearby flats,
the neighbourly flats,
Death seeps —old Dis —from an unancient Stygia

and I head, having made my loop,
noose-shadowed, in bladed blade-grey air
in a guillotine ambience
to my burial,
to the burying-ground of us all

(we will not return the burial grounds,
the ancient, ancestral burying-grounds,
we will return to the burying-grounds
to the burial grounds that will not be there)

to my burial,
to the burial ground for us all —
for no-one
for there is no burial
no lasting city of death

we have here no lasting city,
no lasting city of death:
there shall be no lasting city —
only a drift of ash
where once was a fading incandescent spark

a handful of grey ash drifting,
dispersing,
in the lighted, sightless, universe.

[*Austin — Dallas — Denver*]

I will lie with you
lounging in long grass
on a long mellow afternoon
and twine my fingers in yours
groping in long moist grass;
and then, as the impulse moves,
lock arms, front breasts, touch lips
or lazily tongue, exploring your mouth and tongue

we will lock haunches,
your strong thighs, mobile legs
be active agents to enhance, prolong, delight
and the land slope away to the river-valleys
and rise again in foothills of the far mountains
and the brilliance drain from the bright sky
and the world grow blue, then cold, then dark
and the day go, and night come.

The sand wet and cool
darkening from yellow
to where it was damp,
from a lioness-yellow
to darkness, like ash
or the shadowy underside of a mushroom

and to lounge in such sand,
by the sea, uncaring
scuffing bare heels in the seasand
with the hard ridge of the heel,
half-calloused, half-feeling the cold cool
in warmgold folds, over silkchill skeins

and here to thrust out the legs
to feel the jar in thighflesh and flanks
and through this breakthrough of thighs
to find true fuller freedom of loins and thews
a great freedom of the groin —
an unfolding upflowering of the flesh —

hair uncaring of sand, of shellpowder
broken twigs and dirt;
and to feel the keening of the cold
the ghost of the spray, the spume, the salt —
a cold glitter as of crystals and knives
in the brightness and vagrant warmth of the day:

one assents to the brightness of the day,
its perfection and warmth
acquiescing in the cold in its essence
sharp as a shell-blade and menacing
while the shadows grow long and grey and cold,
one accepts the voluptuous splendour of that day

of an imaginary day
and of an untrue innocent idyll
that never happened
and a perfection of sensuality we never knew
but which they created by report
by alleging this was our act and our guilt:

and straightway
by the evocation of their charge
it was real and true;
and we entered into that sensual idyll
that sunlit sensuous voluptuousness
of luxurious indulgence in lush-ripe flesh:

we were guilty then
accepting the untrue as the real;
so our pursuers, our enemies
became our donors, generous friends:
one perfect sunlit day was ours:
the forbidden idyll became the real:
we had our beach, our sea, our sun,
the stolen sensuous carnal delight
and the spray-bright, spume-chill, bladed air.

[*19 January 1970*]

The archer circles
with poised and twitching finger
while the arrow yearns
nocked and feathered
to go thrilling through the air
and plunge itself in soft flesh —
lose itself in soft flesh —
cease being itself in soft flesh —
to become an other, unnamed,
an ornament and adjunct
blunt, dumb and numb —
no longer the arrowy piercing thing
but merged with the thing it sought out and
        arrowed:

the archer circles
and champs on the earth
a more-than-archer Centaur!

And the beast, the silken beast,
silken flanks dressed
that stamps in the grass,
whose flesh distends, swells, ripples
stertorously
the beast waits
and yearns —
sucks into itself with an embrace of flesh
the arrow
and is sated

While the planets move
to a new auspicious conjunction

Well, let the astral influences rain down
in benign mellifluous streams —
if indeed there are such!

Two persons disport themselves
are arrayed
for this fortuitous deployment —
a perennial balletic jousting
in the panoply of being,
the accretions of circumstance,
and traffic among the bales of time
in the strange barter of dross and glass

Still the sidereal re-assemblies take place,
kaleidoscopic conjunctions unravel,
old bloodshot Aldeberan lowers,
lows, glowers, stumbles into charge
tosses a weary, doomed, beflagged, never-to-be-resting neck —

While Sagitta,
old Sagitta . . .

Sequence
I

Under spotlights
you are more truly a golden goddess
than any other I have known

> (And how can a goddess not be womanly
> nor I, manly
> not find a slow uncurling of power
> along my muscular reaches?)

Poet, you are a pinnacle
of thought, articulation, feeling,
of sensitive perception that laps
into obscurity

and all that my mind calls out for
in idealizing longing
shimmers, by gleams, from your presence

> (How shall the sensual mind, much-travelled
> not rove, speculatively, over your frame,
> imagine postures and abandon?)

Here might be some perfect marriage
of my ideal with you real
and all that wild garden of your experience
of passion, dream and agonized perception
grow to the perfect Mughal landscape

(And my bat-frenzy come to fruit-perfect rest
Atlanta, golden-apple, who but Midas
would presume to eat?
Was not Paris, first consulted, filled with
        fearful amaze?
And I, world-knowledge-saddened, will I
        not forbear?)

II

You will walk, a lambent vision
against black pyramids
of cypresses
over the soft Tuscan hills
against the sapphire Tuscan sky

your foot spurn
the wincing earth
in abstracted anger
and the innocent earth
will bear your scars
long after you are gone.

III

This is an agony I would not wish you
(being devoid of so much malice)
— the discovery of your wrongness
and your wronging of me.

IV

A shot bird
fell from the sky
on the road
with a thud
and gasp
of expiring breath:

I saw the gaping beak
of death
and the gaping mouth
of the torn breast:

some —
fools! —
expected it
to cry out.

V

Oh for a fine anger
and melodramatic phrases
to match yours
— tearing a passion to tatters:

there is a wisdom
wrung from the winepress of long pain
that enables one to see
as in wine turned to amber
all pain as an element
of the matrix of existence.

[155]

VI

I can imagine you blasting a landscape
with thunderbolts
or eclipsing the sun for a company
plunging them into eerie darkness
— cocks crowing in disarray
and bleared stars ghost-walking,
and I am filled with such dismay
thinking what grief you might make
others endure.

VII

There is no magic word
to penetrate
invincible disbelief

and one does not hold up
your crushed heart
in evidence

VIII

The enormity of this offence
(if it were true)
would be a vast columnar umbra
drizzling lethal desolation
over a seismically jagged landscape
a rain of blight and mildew
coruscating over flat worms

a diluvian landscape of morass
thickened slime and blood
spawning frogs locusts and foetuses
corpses impaled on giant thorns
a gloom made of congealed blood
threaded with the high whine of bats

To live thus
with the enormity of the offence
if it were true . . .

A tree, a stone,
a wave, a bird,
have much in common
but nothing relevant;

nor can communicate.
Unheeding, each
squats at its being's centre;
daedal harmonies move them all
but to each other they are dumb:

something, essential, seals us off;
speaking, unhearing, we are out of chord.

[*London*]

You have your private griefs,
I mine:

Peace is not indifference,
nor inaction;
but let us wall ourselves away from war:

Peace comes from inner certitude,
assurance about one's worth
one's status, talents, labours:

and some security, surely
about the nature of things,
directions;

ought we then not to care,
not to share a shared sorrow?

no virtue can transcend charity:
Peace without love is death,
the hollow ribcage of the cadaver.

I could be dead

Be ignorant
Insentiant
Inviolate

lie like a stone
or coffin
under the ground

or stand like a headstone
in the snow
on the earth

with characters engraved
of some assorted past
to dim or fade with weathering

or woodenly, like a coffin
rot and split
with the slow seep of the wet

I could be dead
and ignorantly at ease:
oblivious.

Someday
one will be calm
and temporate
and not cry out in the night
agonizing at memory
and images of sensual delight
that flood over the mind
in waves of satiate balm:
someday
one will escape
the pursuit of lechery
running through the runnels of the mind
in a slow, exquisite and luxuriant play.

Appleford;
the pink blouses fluttering on the clothesline
rusting corrugated iron drums
window frames needing mending

how is a cloistered virtue
possible?
can cloud-layers of academic patois
so insulate?

the return to life's drudgery
is easier
than an eastward swing to London:
how then can you not be aware?

Do not think
the flowers in winter are unmoved

The rosebuds in December
knot

True
the flowers will sway
with every passing breeze
and bend
with a moving stream
or bob
with every heavy drop
that rains down

With the onset of the frost
the rosebuds clench
(those last stubborn strays)
expose chill surfaces —
large shroudlike waxen petals
to shield the tender inner ones,
while by secret regulation
the slow hidden fires of growth
burn
where the lambent colours
exploding perfumes
mature

Deep
to the vast storehouse
of earth's central heat
it reaches
and from the reservoirs of summer's warmth
soaked into passages of the middle earth
it sucks
nuzzling blindly with groping roots
and finds the fire
that flows though thin stem
from vice-gripped roots
to sustain
in tepid warmth
the slow fires of growth,
sempiternal.

Do not think the flowers
are unmoved by the winter's cold:
at the first onset of December frost
the last lingering rosebuds knot

(And what right have we to speak of winter
as a time of cold and death?
We can speak of it
who speak in categories
but cannot speak the Creative Word)

In the frozen heart of winter
in the frost-white air
the world is full of golden berries,
golden and red and bronze and yellow
as the world prepares for next year's birth.

> [*December, 1970. Arthur Nortje, the
> South African poet, died at Oxford
> in this month.*]

Nearby in the park
June's English roses burn
in their soft bright flames of vari-colour
that singe the eyes, the nostrils, senses:

the clear night air
clear from the window, clearer in the mirror
that crystals images to dreamlike Italianate
        purity
comes home to the central essence of the self,
        mind,
                feeling that we call heart:

suddenly the world is real,
the self stands poised and conscious at a
        central point;
awareness, sensation, the welter of things
is stripped of its burden, anguish, and abrasive
        barbs.

Country and continent
how you devour

and how desire ravages,
yeasts queasily in my guts
uncoils along my entrails and my loins.

August's late-summer roses swell and blow,
preen lustrous vermilions and plumflesh blood-
     reds
thrust and expose for public open secret rose
discoloured inwardness and rank pungent scents:

appetite lunges at my loins
clutches and gouges at my crotch.

In late-summer
in the many-scented air
with early leaffalls drifting;
in the muddled air
in my perturbed, questing, arguing,
perturbed and troubled mind;
my ageing, flagging, earthward-turning mind
with sap running low in the flesh,
settled ways mossing around the heart,
appetites blunting to a dull lift of the flesh

country and continent
how you devour.

And in the mouldring unclear days
I must quest, troubled,
for an answer
to the fierce insensate impulses
that drive me out in paroxysms of desire
— insatiable, unappeasable,
unsatisfiable desire.

Country and continent
how you are subsumed,
a succubus-femalemess
whose contours, hollows, cradled all my lust
and whose uninterruptable urge
drags on me now
sucks on my energies
and steers me homeward to the familiar nest.

August's late-summer roses preen
their lustrous yellows now
imperiously.

Does the heart survive the death of love

the slow receding of the flush of tenderness
leaving wet sand and debris,
dessicated shards of molluscs
the stink of decaying weed and fish

the slow atrophy of the fibrils of tenderness
leaving a numbness
and scarred dead-white tissue
a keratinous scaling and gangrenous rot

vision grows lack-lustre glaucous,
cloud-lour darkens the sun, cloud, skies,
colours are leached to nondescript shades;
pulse thickens and rigor freezes the limbs:

love being dead, or dying, can the heart survive?

[*London*]

For Chief

A Tribute
to
Albert John Luthuli

died
July, 1967

1

So the old leonine heart is stilled

the grave composure of the carven face
matched at last by a stillness overall

the measure of bitterness, totally filled
brims to the tautness of exhausted space

and he who sustained a faith in grace
believing men crippled could still walk tall
in the thorn-thickets of corrupting power

and more dear the central humanity
than any abstractions of time or place
daring to challenge, refusing to cower

mangled even at the end, he lies quiet
his stillness no less an assertion of faith
and the indestructible stubbornness of will.

2

So the machine breaks you
and you fall
still fighting grimly

the years epitomize
in this harsh act
of many:

Should one despair
knowing how great the power
how unavailing opposition?

Yet your great soul
asserts a worth —
transcendant humanity.

There is a valour
greater than victory:
　　Greatness endures.

3

And the people mourn
the millions mourn,
the sorrowing land
is plunged in deeper sorrow:

When will the soft rains dissolve the entire landscape
        at dusk?

Sorrow and anger stir,
Dull pain and truculent woe,
and bitterness slowly seethes
till fury cauldrons from pain —

Oh when will the blind storms rampage the landscape in
        the dark?

4

Return to us

when sunset smoulders on the smooth horizon,
when the trees are starkly black
and beautiful
against the red and mauve of the sky

Return to us

when woodsmoke comes sweet and poignant
from the fields at dusk
after the winds of our fury have breathed
on the smouldering coals of our anger
and our fierce destruction has raged

O great patient enduring spirit
return to us.

5

O grave and statuesque man
stand along our paths,
overlook our ways

goad us by your calm regard
fire us with your desire,
steel us with your will.

Spirit of freedom and courage
guard us from despair
brood over us with your faith.

Fire the flagging and the faint,
spur us to fierce resolve,
drive us to fight and win.

6

And you
my friends
my allies
cosily chaired in London
or termiting in a thousand towns
or treadmilling the arid round
of protest, picket, pamphlet —
for as long as fervour lasts:
what shall I say of us?

O let Chief's reflected splendour
and the aura resistance sometimes brings —
except to the jaded, jaundiced, cynic —
o let us catch a little of this fire
and let us burn and steadily assert
our faith, our will to freedom and our love
for freedom and our dear unhappy land:
of inextinguishable and hungry fire
of love and hunger and imperishable resolve.

7

And the men
the dear lonely men
gaunt, and with a hunger around the eyes,
and the busy women
friendly strangers in a hundred lands:
ah these, my comrades and my friends!
how long, oh how much longer must it be?
how long still the wrench at throat
the pluck at eyes
at mention of some small forgotten word —
Fietas or Woodstock or Gelvandale —?
how much longer must we doggedly importune
in the anterooms of governors of the world
or huddle stubborn on the draughty frontiers of
      strange lands?
how long must we endure?
and how shall I express my gratitude and love?

[*Kitwe, Lusaka, Nairobi, London July 1967*]

A simple lust is all my woe:
the thin thread of agony
that runs through the reins
after the flesh is overspent
in over-taxing acts of love:

only I speak the others' woe:
those congealed in concrete
or rotting in rusted ghetto-shacks;
only I speak their wordless woe,
their unarticulated simple lust.

[*December 1971*]